WHO TURNED OUT THE LIGHTS?!

Finding Treasure in Life's Dark Places

WHO TURNED OUT THE LIGHTS?!

Finding Treasure in Life's Dark Places

by

Candy Reid

Wyatt House Publishing
www.wyattpublishing.com

Wyatt House books may be ordered through booksellers or by contacting:

WYATT HOUSE PUBLISHING
399 Lakeview Dr. W.
Mobile, Alabama 36695
www.wyattpublishing.com

Because of the dynamic nature of the Internet, any web address or links contained in this book may have changed since publication and may no longer be valid. The views expressed in this book are solely those of the author and do not necessarily reflect those of the publisher, and the publisher hereby disclaims any responsibility for them.

Cover design by: Mark Wyatt and Mary Ann Wyatt
Author photo courtesy of: Joshua Reid

ISBN 13 TP: 978-0-9882209-4-2
Library of Congress Control Number: 2012954821

Printed in the United States of America

Dedication

This book is lovingly dedicated to
the family and friends who so
selflessly ministered to our
family during our darkest of days.

Thank you.

I will give you the treasures of darkness. And hidden riches of secret places, that you may know that I, the LORD, Who call you by your name, I Am the God of Israel.

Isaiah 45:3

Darkness. I've experienced my fair share of it. If you've lived any length of time, I'm sure you have as well. And, like me, you can probably recall with more clarity than you'd like the moments that snuffed out the light of the sun. You know them, those moments in our existence that are so forever life changing that there could never be any way to simply dismiss the memory. How could the heart break of hearing the words "I don't love you anymore" or the breath-taking fear caused when a doctor declares, "You have cancer" ever be forgotten? Could our minds ever truly obliterate the memory of our emotional response to the death of a loved one - the ocean of despair that threatens to overtake every part of our mind, body, and spirit? How could we forget the rock-in-your-stomach realization that a precious child has rejected years of truth to pursue destruction? These and other such junctures in life's journey pivot us toward travels into the darkness of places unknown, forcing us to leave behind sunshiny days; wondering if we'll ever find our way back to the light.

It seemed that one minute I'd be minding my own business, enjoying all the goodness that life can bring, and then suddenly, outta nowhere, POOF! All semblance of light was extinguished and darkness descended. I'm sure that God must have wanted to put His fingers in His ears when I wailed "Why me?!" for the thousandth time.

It was when I finally (after many tears and not a few pity parties) allowed God to change my outlook from "Why me?!" to "Why *not* me?" that I was able to receive the treasures that my precious heavenly Father wanted to give me as a direct result of having walked in the darkness.

How selfish it would be of me to hoard those treasures for myself! The sole purpose of this book is to share some of those treasures with you. It's my prayer that as you read my heart on the following pages you'll find encouragement and strength for your journey.

We know that all things work together for good to those who love God: those who are the called according to His purpose.

Romans 8:28

Few things have the ability to strike fear in the heart of new parents like a toddler's rapidly rising temperature. My husband Randy and I discovered this first hand when our second son, Joshua, was a tot. Just about any time that child got sick, and he seemed to do that quite a bit, his fever would sky-rocket. We made many frantic, but completely unnecessary trips to the emergency room; thoroughly convinced that our precious bundle of joy was surely suffering from one rare disease or another. After one such late night hospital visit at which Joshua was again diagnosed with some common childhood ailment, Randy and I decided that we should work on incorporating some more practical steps at home the next time our little guy's fever started spiking.

It wasn't long before we were given the opportunity to try our hand at bringing down a quickly climbing temperature. Although we administered Tylenol at the onset of the fever his body showed no response to the medicine. As usual, his temp continued to rise. Next we gave him a dose of Ibuprofen; another 20 minute wait and a recheck. Still, the fever was rapidly passing 103 degrees. Our plan was in place. The nurse's instructions were: Simply place Joshua into a tub of tepid water. Pour water over his little fevered body. Wait for it to evaporate. Repeat this simple process for 20 minutes or until his fever started to come down. Sounded easy enough. We could do this, right?

Unfortunately, few things are as easy as they sound. The 'cool, but not *too* cool water' felt like ice to his fevered skin. Joshua's reaction left no doubt that this wasn't happening without a fight. No way was he going to let us torture him without major resistance. The screaming, thrashing, splashing, and crying that ensued had me convinced that concerned neighbors would soon be calling the police. All the while, Randy and I were doing our best to stay calm - speaking gently to him, telling him we loved him, explaining that this had to be done and it was good for him. He was not at *all* interested in what we had to say. He'd be still long enough to hold his little hands up, fully expecting to be lifted into our arms. With tears streaming down his chubby cheeks there was no mistaking the confusion in his big blue eyes when we'd tell him that we couldn't get him out. Even though he couldn't communicate with words, the expression on his face and the frustration in his cries clearly said, "Why won't you just pick me up?!"

Oh, how I wanted to do just that! But, in spite of what he thought, I knew that taking him out of that terrible, 'tortuous' situation would do more harm than good. I wanted so badly for him to understand that his fighting was only making the situation more difficult and was actually prolonging what could have been a fairly quick process. But my words were beyond his ability to understand. He wanted less talk and more action!

I remember as vividly as if it were yesterday the Holy Spirit speaking to my heart at that moment and teaching me that I had so often done the same thing with Him. So many times in life when I'd had to endure painful, uncomfortable situations I had fought and questioned, furious that the God who could simply 'pick me up' would choose not to do so. Instead of trusting Him, believing that He was allowing ALL things to work for my good, I would assume that He didn't care about what I was enduring. In that moment I realized that just as I was longing for Joshua to trust that we would never allow him to face such discomfort if there wasn't a very needful purpose, I needed to trust that my heavenly Father would never allow me to endure what would not ultimately bring about my good. I understood with startling clarity that He who is infinitely more wise and loving than any earthly parent would never leave me in a dark, uncomfortable place any longer than was absolute necessary. I had no way of knowing what trials lay ahead, but the truth that was birthed in my spirit that night as we struggled with a very unhappy toddler has encouraged me through many dark places.

Treasure: Trust that our heavenly Father would never allow you to suffer needlessly. He truly will work all things for your good as you submit yourself to His care.

Trust in the Lord with all your heart, and lean not on your own understanding...

Proverbs 3:5

In 2003 life was good. After 13 years of renting we had recently bought our first house...a cute little place in the country with a swimming pool for the hot summer days and an acre of woods where 3 rambunctious boys could play and build forts. We had 4 healthy children. Little Sarah, our newest addition, was only a year old. We were actively serving at a wonderful church; Randy was the associate pastor and worship leader while I played the piano and took a turn teaching children's church every few weeks. Our faith in God was strong and solid.

One fall morning (Tuesday, October 28 at 7:35 a.m. to be exact) everything changed. The day started out routinely enough. I had gotten up early to fix Randy's breakfast and spend some time with him before he went to work. After Randy left I decided to get a bit more rest before waking the kids. Our youngest son, Zay, who was 3 at that time, climbed into bed with me. We'd only been in bed for a short time when he started hitting me in the back. Now, hitting mama in the back wasn't something that was normally done. I was feeling none too happy that he'd decided to use the few minutes I had to rest as a time to test a new boundary. I turned over to find out what was causing his temporary lapse in sanity only to find him staring into space with his mouth slightly open and his arms and legs jerking violently. He was making a horrible gasping noise and drool was slowly trickling down his chin. It was like nothing I'd ever seen. I started shaking him and calling his name, but he wouldn't respond. The drooling, gasping, and jolting would not stop. My brain couldn't process what was happening. "Why won't he respond to me? He must be choking. Why won't he blink? I need to turn him over. How can he be so stiff when every part of his body is jerking?" Those and a dozen other disjointed thoughts assailed my mind. And then slowly I realized, "He's having a seizure." The helplessness I felt at that moment was indescribable. A call to 911 brought the ambulance. It took them f.o.r.e.v.e.r. to get to our house out in the country and little Zay's body continued to spasm violently until moments before the EMTs came into my room.

Randy, my parents, our pastor and some other church members met us at the hospital. We were there for hours; the hospital staff performing what tests they could with limited resources. (I wasn't feeling so fond of "country life" right about then.) We were to have no answers that day.

The drive home was quiet. Zay's glassy stare, a lingering effect of the havoc his brain had wreaked on his body, mirrored the emotions that I felt. I was almost numb. Silent tears streamed down my cheeks as my spirit challenged me to trust in God. As the sounds of Third Day's "Offering" drifted softly through our van I knew my spirit was querying the question, "Will you trust?" In my heart I offered Zay to God…choosing to trust.

Treasure: Trusting is always easier when life's at its best and you're surrounded by sunshine and roses. There's a reason Solomon admonishes his readers to trust in the Lord with "all your heart". He knew that sometimes a reminder would be necessary. God's Word settled deeply within your spirit will resurface to sustain and strengthen you even in the most challenging of times.

*About midnight Paul and Silas were praying and
singing hymns to God, and the prisoners were
listening to them.*
Acts 16:25

Twelve days later Zay had another seizure.
After that he had them daily; some days he would
have just one and other days he would have
dozens. He not only had the violent grand-mal
seizures, he started having quick 'drop attacks'. The
drop attacks only lasted long enough to knock him
to the floor, but they were very dangerous. The
misfiring in his brain hit like lightening, slamming
every part of his body at once. He would make a
sharp exhale noise that was caused from the air

being forced out of his lungs and then he'd hit the floor or fall off the potty or hit his head on the table. Eventually he was required to wear a custom-made helmet for his protection. He would often have clusters of seizures with no rest for his body between multiple seizures resulting in a serious medical emergency. Valium suppositories were always on hand to use to stop the clusters or to use if a grand-mal continued longer than 2 minutes. He was deteriorating cognitively as well. Before seizures he was fairly advanced for a 3 year old, sounding out words and working simple math problems. Epilepsy robbed him of the ability to recall letter names and sounds or even remember how to count to 10.

During these months we were, of course, seeing specialists and searching for answers. We had to see several neurologists before finally getting a correct diagnosis: myoclonic astatic epilepsy (MAE). The neurologists tried several different medicines at different doses. Sometimes the seizure activity would lessen, but it did not stop and it was always a matter of time before the frequency increased again. Treatment such as the Ketogenic diet that was known to combat this particular seizure syndrome was not even an option for Zay because of an irregular seizure presentation. The prognosis we were given at the time was very frightening.

Cases were reported of children with MAE who had suddenly stopped having seizures and returned to normal, but if certain criteria were present then the chances of 'spontaneous recovery' appeared to be virtually non-existent. Zay exhibited the majority of those criteria. Faced with the cold, hard facts and armed with the information our neurologist offered, we were seriously considering surgery to remove the offending part of Zay's brain.

How had we ended up here...in *this* dark place? Is there any darker place than helplessly watching your child suffer? Well-meaning people would tell me stories of how they had faced terrible situations and how God, "because of their faith", had turned everything around instantly. Were they implying that my faith wasn't strong enough?

Let me be transparent and offer you a glimpse into the heart of a mama who had cried out to God continually **knowing** that He was able to heal Zay, a mama who was weary from seeing absolutely no physical evidence that a healing was taking place. I wanted to scream in their religious, well-meaning faces, "I HAVE faith!!" But, of course, I did not. Instead I would simply smile under the weight of their unwitting condemnation knowing that any words I offered in defense of my faith would appear foolish in light of Zay's obvious deterioration.

But in the quiet hours of the night when the constant listening for the sound of another seizure from Zay's little bed next to ours kept my mind from any true rest, I began to wonder....What if I *don't* have enough faith? Am I *really* praying hard enough? Maybe, if I just prayed harder or believed stronger I could move the heart of God to step in and save my son. Was there some unconfessed sin for which I was being punished? Could it be that desperate searching of my heart would eventually reveal secret rebellion? Maybe that was the key…extracting that sin and eradicating it. Then, surely then, God would hear my prayers and move on our behalf.

Mercifully, God did not ignore my anguish.

I was compelled to look to His Word for answers. In Acts 16 I read the amazing account of two people, Paul and Silas, doing their best to do what God had told them to do. God had given Paul a vision and told him to go Macedonia. Paul "immediately" made preparations and started the journey. After he and Silas arrived in Philippi (in Macedonia), they were on their way to prayer when they encountered, not for the first time, a girl possessed by demons. She needed freedom, so they cast out the demons in the name of Jesus. You'd think everyone in town would be ecstatic about the girl's miraculous deliverance, but that's not what happened. Paul and Silas were attacked, dragged to the marketplace to face the town authorities, beaten with rods, thrown into the inner part of a prison and put in chains.

What?!

Based on what I read in God's Word I had to ask a new set of questions. Could it be that sometimes we're doing the best we know to do and stuff just happens? Is it possible that horrible things happen as a result of living in a fallen world? Didn't Jesus tell us in John 16:33 that we would have tribulation?

Thankfully a prison stint wasn't the end of the story for Paul and Silas. These two men, who seemed to have every right to shake their fist at God and demand answers, made a choice to praise God even in the darkness of undeserved imprisonment. The other prisoners heard their praise and, more importantly, God heard their praise. God showed Himself mighty in their situation by shaking the prison and causing everyone's chains to fall off and the doors of the prison to be opened. The jailer and the members of his house were saved. Paul and Silas were given a platform from which to shout God's praises that would not have been available to them had it not been for the sufferings they endured. The salvation of the jailer, his household, and, I'm sure many of the prisoners, was a direct result of the way Paul and Silas chose to handle their tribulation. They chose to believe that God is worthy of praise even in the darkest of places.

During the dark days of Zay's illness I too decided that God is worthy of my praise no matter the situation or the circumstance - even if Zay never recovered on this side of heaven and my destiny was to spend the rest of my life caring for a child who was unable to care for himself. It was a new 'faith place' for me. I realized that the God who loved me enough to send His Son to die for my sins would not withhold valuable information that would be the key to my son's recovery. Even if Zay wasn't healed I would still choose to trust that God would work this situation for our good and for His glory just as He did for Paul and Silas and those around them.

Treasure: Trust that God, in His perfect timing, will fulfill purposes and plans for you that are beyond what you can see now. If you're willing, even the most difficult of places can be used as a platform from which to declare God's praises.

Come to Me, all you who labor and are heavy laden,
and I will give you rest.

Matthew 11:28

I'd love to tell you that once I chose to trust God with Zay's illness I never questioned or grew weary; that I was always smiling and full of peace. But I won't because it would be a lie. Even though Zay required constant attention I still had three other children who needed a mama. We were still homeschooling, the floors still needed to be mopped, meals didn't cook themselves, and Randy's job required him to be away from home for ridiculously long hours. Sarah was a toddler and she was into e.v.e.r.y.t.h.i.n.g. (her favorite form of entertainment was playing in her poop every time she had the chance. As if I didn't have enough to do without having to clean poop out of her ears, nose and belly button!). Some days were so stressful that I honestly thought I would lose my mind.

At the end of one particularly long day I was preparing to give Zay his night time meds when I realized that Sarah had once again explored the contents of her diaper. I put away the medicines to handle the task of de-pooping Sarah and her room. (If only I could undo the mess as fast as she made it!) After depositing a freshly-bathed Sarah into her daddy's arms and disinfecting her bedroom walls and floor, I was finally ready to give Zay his meds and begin bedtime preparations - again. I wearily retrieved the medicine from the locked-box in the kitchen, carried it to where Zay was waiting with daddy and Sarah and in what can only be explained as the result of a brain that was pushed almost to the point of no return, promptly told Sarah to "Open up!" She did and I squirted the first dose of medicine right into her sweet little mouth. Immediately I realized my mistake...but it was too late. She had swallowed and the medicine had already made its way into her tiny little tummy. Now this wasn't the equivalent of giving a child the wrong dose of Tylenol, which would have been horrible enough. I had just given my toddler a ridiculously high dose of anti-seizure medicine that could only be safely given to Zay because we had gradually increased the amount given over a 2 week period under the direction and supervision of a neurologist. This was HUGE! I-may-have-killed-my-child HUGE!

After a frantic call to poison control, we made a fast-as-we-could-get-there trip to the emergency room for medical observation. After a long night at the ER she was fine.

I, on the other hand, was not fine. To say that I was struggling with guilt would be the understatement of the century. In the wee hours of that morning I found myself painfully aware of my inadequacies. And though I was too weary to even call out to Him, God heard the silent cries of my heart. He reminded me of the rest that He offered. I recognized that this rest, the kind that could prevail even in the face of such trying circumstances and allow clarity of thought in a mama as frazzled as me, would not be encountered by chance. It would come as I intentionally chose to carve out moments, fleeting though they would sometimes have to be, to spend with Him. Strength for the journey and the mental ability to walk through this dark place would only be found by allowing my spirit and mind to rest in Christ even when the physical demands of the day could not be denied.

Treasure: The clamor of this world and the very real needs that surround us call for our constant attention, but intentional time spent with God will allow Him the opportunity to gift us with true rest…restoring our minds, bodies and spirits.

Be anxious for nothing, but in everything by prayer and supplication, with thanksgiving, let your requests be made known to God; and the peace of God, which surpasses all understanding, will guard your hearts and minds through Christ Jesus.

Philippians 4: 6, 7

At one point, several months after the seizures started Zay went eight days without any seizure activity. We just knew he was healed and we were proclaiming the wonderful news to anyone who would listen. Randy encouraged me to go on a ladies retreat our church was hosting, ensuring me that he could hold down the fort. There was no question that I needed the break and since I knew Zay was fine I agreed to go. Friday night at the retreat was amazing! Wonderful fellowship, great food, uplifting Word. I went to bed feeling refreshed and looking forward to Saturday.

How could I know that Saturday morning would dawn with a frantic phone call shattering my hope for Zay's healing?

But the call did come. It was Randy...Zay was having a seizure - the type that mercilessly jerked his body for minutes at a time. I sat devastated with the phone to my ear offering silent support to a daddy whose heart was just as crushed as mine. Finally the calming effects of the valium that Randy had administered made their way through Zay's little system and he was able to sleep the deep sleep that came after a seizure had ravaged his body. I knew that there was nothing I could do to change the situation, but somehow I couldn't stand the thought of not being with Zay. I packed to go home. But Randy insisted that I stay through to the end of the retreat. After all, he reasoned, he could handle things as well as I could. I hung up the phone and knew that, once again, I had a choice to make. Would I trust God? I decided I would choose to trust. With tears streaming down my cheeks I actually declared out loud, "I will trust my God." There are simply no words to describe the amazingly sweet fellowship that I experienced with God during our worship time that afternoon.

Back at home, things continued on a path that we were beginning to consider normal, and unfortunately that included seizures. One afternoon Zay had a particularly violent seizure. When it was over I held him in my lap and snuggled him closely knowing that it would be a while before he recovered. I wanted him to be in my arms when his consciousness began the groggy search for reality. But his brain refused to allow him to rest. Over the next hour he had more than a dozen seizures. All the while I was praying, asking God to make. them. stop...NOW! Can I be real with you? I was beyond angry. Forget all the 'trust' stuff...I wanted my child healed. Not later. Right NOW. My heart was breaking and I decided at that moment that I was through praying. Why bother when God was going to do what He wanted no matter how many times I asked or how many tears I cried? I went to bed that night with a very icy heart.

God, in His infinite wisdom recognized that my heart wasn't truly rebellious, simply shattered. Off and on the next day I felt the Holy Spirit stirring my heart, quietly asking me to trust, reminding me of the refuge I'd find in Him. I resisted, stubbornly holding on to my anger. Throughout the day He gently persisted. As I read to the kids, washed dishes, fixed lunches, and woodenly did all the things that moms do every day, scriptures swirled in my mind gently calling me back. It was while I was doing my least favorite chore - folding clothes - that I felt the Holy Spirit stir my heart with the words of Philippians 4: 6, 7. Slowly I allowed the ice around my heart to thaw under the warmth of His words. As if He was just waiting for the moment that I would be willing to allow Him to speak to my heart I was suddenly filled with the revelation of just how those words applied to me...right where I was.

I had always understood that scripture to mean that God's peace surpassed my ability to comprehend. At the Holy Spirit's prompting I realized that if I was willing to permit my heart and mind to move past the need to understand the 'why' of what was happening in our lives and the 'when' of Zay's healing then I could experience true peace. Peace that could only be acquired in a place that passed my understanding. Don't get me wrong, I wasn't delusional. I didn't think that God changed the meaning of a scripture just to meet my need, but I KNEW that He opened my heart to grasp exactly what I desperately needed at that moment...another call to rest in Him, to trust Him even if nothing was happening as I thought it should, to experience the peace that could only be found in Him. He gave me another treasure in a very dark place. And my grateful heart has guarded it faithfully ever since.

Treasure: Being able to accept silence when we're asking questions whose answers are so desperately important to us is unbelievably difficult. I don't think for one moment that God ever lacks the answers, but I do know from experience that sometimes those answers simply aren't going to come in the time or form that we want. I urge you to trust God enough to be willing to allow your heart and mind to move past the need to understand. Lay your unanswered questions at His feet and take on His peace - the peace that truly does surpass all understanding.

Therefore God also has highly exalted Him and given
Him the name which is above every name...

Philippians 2:9

Though the years of Zay's illness were long and painful his seizures did eventually begin to slow and then, finally - blessedly, stop. He had his last seizure on January 2, 2006. It was a violent drop attack that happened while he was standing in our living room. The force of the seizure sent him backward across the room; almost as if the sickness was making its 'last stand'. Slowly he began to regain that which had been lost. Social skills, academic milestones, physical abilities that had eluded him for so long began to be realized. During the fall of 2007 our neurologist felt comfortable weaning Zay off of his last anti-seizure medicine. This was done gradually over a 6 week period while we observed him carefully for any signs of a setback. Finally in October 2007 Zay was seizure free AND medicine free. At almost 8 years old he learned to tie his shoes, ride a bike, grasp a pencil, and catch a ball. He was able to understand the academic concepts that had previously been beyond his grasp and he was well on his way to being considered 'grade level'.

Miraculously, today you would never believe that Zay's mind and body had endured those terrible years. There are no obvious traces of the dreaded MAE. I liken it to the three Hebrew children who were thrown into the fire and came out without even having the smell of smoke on their clothes (you can check out their story in Daniel chapter 3).

One month after Zay swallowed his last dose of anti-seizure medicine I found a lump in my left breast. A very tiny, almost undetectable, English pea-sized lump. So small, in fact, that I didn't feel the need to see a doctor, but Randy was adamant that I have it checked.

The next two weeks were a whirl-wind of doctors' visits, trips to the hospital, ultrasounds, mammograms, and more pokes and prods than I ever thought possible. Add to that the unexpected death of my mother-in-law and the news that, though the tests results still weren't back, the now rapidly growing lump was "likely" cancer. My nerves were shot.

Emotions I thought I had long since surrendered to God rose to the surface...fear and anger leading the pack. I mean, really?! Hadn't we been through enough? I tried to pray; to turn this fear of cancer over to the One who could carry the burden for me, but my prayers were disjointed and sporadic. I couldn't seem to focus very long on forming prayers. My mind was much too busy. My thoughts and emotions were consumed with the ache of losing a loved one, the financial burden of planning a funeral with no insurance, the daunting task of having a little over a week to clean out my mother-in-law's home before we would be required to pay another month's rent, a grieving husband who needed me (though his desire to be strong for me wouldn't allow him to admit it), doctor and hospital appointments that had to be kept, little ones who were struggling with the loss of their grandma, and a teenager who was quite certain that the world still revolved around him. Throw in the "what if's" that constantly bombarded my mind and I was completely unable to corral my thoughts long enough to make any sort of intelligible plea to God.

Mercifully, God knew my heart and honored my pitiful attempts at communication. He whispered to my spirit a wonderful reminder of the words of Philippians 2:9...Jesus has been given the name that is above ALL names. Even if that name is the dreaded "cancer".

When the results of the biopsy did, in fact, name the offending lump cancer and fear desired to overwhelm me I chose to trust that my Jesus is above (beyond, across, instead of, superior to, more than) cancer. And though my voice would tremble with uncertainty at times, I chose to declare this treasure from a dark place to anyone who would listen.

Treasure: Trust that the very name of Jesus is above anything you're facing. If you can name it, loneliness, cancer, unemployment, confusion… anything, He is above it. And He is well able to deliver you from it or take you through it all the while working things for your good and His glory.

You will keep him in perfect peace, whose mind is stayed on You, because he trusts in You.

Isaiah 26:3

Things moved very quickly once we realized that the lump was indeed a malignant tumor. I learned that the cancer invading my body was a fairly uncommon, very aggressive type known as triple negative (TN) breast cancer. I don't know of advancements that may have been made in the medical community since my diagnosis, but at the time I was not given a very hopeful prognosis. Most breast cancers have one of three specific receptors: estrogen, progesterone, or HER2. There are specific chemotherapies used to target these receptors to stop the growth of the cancerous cells. A diagnosis of TN meant that the tumor in my body did not possess any of the above mentioned receptors and therefore treatment would be much more challenging.

After much prayer, Randy and I decided to participate in a clinical trial; trusting that God would allow me to be randomized to the exact arm of the trial that would be best for me. The randomization afforded me the opportunity to receive 2 chemotherapy drugs that had not yet been approved for treatment in TN patients. These were given in addition to the traditional treatment whose results had been less than promising. But, they also came with some very unpleasant side effects. I was warned that the next few months would NOT be a walk in the park.

There was so much to take in. I was bombarded with information everywhere I turned. I needed more hospital visits for extra tests to ensure that my body could handle the added burden of additional chemotherapy. A port to be used as the entrance for the cancer killing drugs was placed in my chest. I attended pre-chemo education so that I could be prepared for what was to come (as if!). Everything had to be done quickly as the tumor was growing at a ridiculously fast rate. Just a few weeks after its initial discovery the once tiny lump was now large enough for others to notice even when I was wearing a baggy sweatshirt! It didn't take me long at all to realize that allowing my thoughts to dwell on the upcoming battle for any length of time would render me almost paralyzed with anxiety – the elephant-sitting-on-your-chest, can't-breathe kind of anxiety.

Turning that trepidation over to God by keeping my mind on Him (reading His Word, listening to Godly counsel, praying) was the only effective weapon that I could wield to wage war against the foreboding that threatened to smother the life out of me. As I focused my thoughts on Him and the truths found in His Word, my mind was once again able to embrace peace in a place that defied placidity.

Treasure: Keeping our thoughts firmly fixed on God during times of chaos and uncertainty is the only way we can be assured of true and lasting peace.

Therefore humble yourselves under the mighty hand of God, that He may exalt you in due time, casting all your care upon Him, for He cares for you.

I Peter 5: 6, 7

Although I found peace by resting in the knowledge that God was in control of my life even when it seemed very out of control there was one area that was still causing me a great deal of struggle - my children. I always said that I trusted God with my children (and I really believed myself), but this situation forced me to face the realization that I only trusted God with them if I was in control of their care. While I knew the family or the few close friends who would be stepping in to help in this area would never purposely harm my kids, I still had some major concerns. I remember lying in my bed, crying quietly so I wouldn't wake Randy and telling God how frightened I was of letting others take care of the kids. "What if they aren't as patient as I would be? Will they be able to recognize Sarah's sweet heart beyond all of her busyness? What if they don't realize that Joshua's struggling inside even though he seems fine on the outside? What if they ignore Zay because Sarah demands so much attention? Will Caleb get lost in the shuffle because he's the oldest and is expected to handle this 'like a man'?" And on and on I went questioning God and explaining to Him why I couldn't relinquish the care of our children to anyone else even for short periods of time.

Then softly I felt the Holy Spirit speak to my heart reminding me that my children were His before they were mine. As great as my love was for my children, His was even greater. I learned that if I would be willing to humble myself, recognizing that He was well able to handle placing my children with the right person for each situation, and cast even these most important of all cares onto Him then He would certainly be faithful to ensure their needs would be met.

Treasure: Pride in our ability to handle any situation ourselves will keep us from trusting it completely to God. We really *can* cast all of our cares on Him because He truly does care for us and for the concerns of our heart.

*And He said to me, "My grace is sufficient for you,
for My strength is made perfect in weakness."*

II Corinthians 12: 9

It didn't take very long for my body to begin exhibiting many of the side effects I was warned about. Indescribably painful mouth sores, debilitating exhaustion, bleeding issues, prickly pain on the bottoms of my feet, dangerously low white blood cell counts, and eventually nausea, and rotting, painful fingernails were all part of the chemo package.

On the emotional side I found that, in spite of previously won spiritual battles, fear, doubt, worry, and discouragement all desired to be my constant companions. The physical aspects of exhaustion, insomnia (in spite of the exhaustion), and pain were real and could not be ignored. I had children who still needed a mama. I couldn't clean house or cook, but I could focus my energy on homeschooling my kids. I tried to keep things as 'routine' as possible. We did have to make some changes; working around hospital visits and pre-planning lessons to be overseen by someone else if needed. My over-organized, time-enslaved self also found that our school day could start at 10:00 or 11:00 just as well as 8:30 and I could handle many subjects with the little ones right in my bed (they didn't mind that a bit). We had a plan in place for the really rough days - the kids knew that if I closed my eyes during a lesson they needed to be really quiet for a few minutes while I worked through the pain.

I quickly learned that the only way I could survive the journey called 'cancer' would be if I surrendered every part of me to Christ over and over again. In no way could I lean on my own strength...to try to do so only magnified how very weak I was. There were times when the old motto "one day at a time" was too overwhelming. I learned to walk "one moment at a time". And I found that His grace was sufficient.

Treasure: Any weakness in your life, once surrendered to Christ, can be used as a way to highlight the sufficiency of God's grace to equip you with the means to handle even the most difficult of circumstances. Even if some days dictate that surrender happen over and over again.

But if a woman has long hair it is a glory to her...

I Corinthians 11:15

Not every type of chemotherapy causes the loss of hair. But, wouldn't you know it...of the six different drugs I would be getting two were guaranteed to cause hair loss. One of those drugs would be given during the first four cycles of treatment and the other during the second four cycles. So, in preparation for the inevitable I had my waist length hair cut to my shoulders. I reasoned it would be easier to care for during the coming weeks anyway. It was actually kind of cute...in a naturally curly, do-your-own-thing kind of way. Whenever I'd start to feel apprehensive about the new bald look that I'd soon be sporting I would simply remind myself to focus on the bigger picture. In the scheme of things 'hairless' shouldn't be that big of a deal. "After all," I reasoned, "It's just hair. It'll grow back."

One afternoon a few weeks after my first chemo treatment my tresses began their exodus, slowly at first - in my hand as I absentmindedly ran my fingers through my curls; on the pillow after a nap; in the tub after a bath. Judging by the massive clumps of hair that were turning up everywhere it seemed that I would be completely bald in a day or two, but the loss continued in earnest over the period of several days. I guess I expected to just wake up one morning and be bald. I didn't realize that it would be a process that would start with patches of scalp peeking past the clumps of hair that were determined to hang on. The thought of looking like I had the mange was too much for me. The pitiful remains had to go. It was when I got out our handy-dandy home hair cutting kit that I discovered I had given myself way too much credit - I was not at all prepared for this. There are no words to adequately express the emotions that I felt. My body had betrayed me and now my bald head would declare it for all the world to see. I couldn't do it. I could not shave off the rest of my hair. Randy, my knight in shining armor, came to my rescue. He would do the dirty work.

I found that none of us were really ready. My sister came to our house, just to be near. Caleb told me later that he cried. Randy was uncharacteristically quiet. I didn't realize until much later the heavy toll the sight of my baldness would exact from my husband's heart. It was an everyday, in-your-face reminder that he who did not take lightly his role as protector and guardian in our family was helpless to stop cancer's forward march.

I stood watching in the mirror as Randy gently ran the buzzer over my head. As the endless supply of tears steadily made their way down my cheeks my weary spirit whispered a question...Could I possibly consider this an exchanging of my glory (hair) for His glory (praise for Him in every circumstance)? Though it would not be easy, I decided that was exactly how I would choose to walk out this part of my cancer journey. The shift in the tide of my emotions wasn't immediate, but I was able to trust, by faith, that any exchange offered in sacrifice to God would bring forth good.

   Treasure: Any sacrifice that we're required to make can ultimately be used to bring about our good and His glory.

Finally, brethren, whatever things are true, whatever
things are noble, whatever things are just, whatever
things are pure, whatever things are lovely, whatever
things are of good report, if there is any virtue and if
there is anything praiseworthy—
meditate on these things.

Philippians 4:8

The chemotherapy and all the nasty side effects did, of course, come to an end. But this did not signal the end of cancer's consequence for my body. One month after my last treatment I was scheduled to have a bilateral mastectomy. Shortly after my diagnosis I had declared with the arrogance of the ignorant that losing a breast wouldn't be that difficult. After all, it's just a breast.

Who knew I'd end up losing not just one, but both to a surgeon's knife? How could I have known the emotions that would be involved in losing something so seemingly insignificant? I found that I was not at all prepared to face the operating room.

I was too close to the situation to find any way to tangibly express my raw emotions. How could I communicate in a concrete way that which did not make sense even to me? Looking back I realize that, among other things, I was grieving the loss of part of myself. Maybe they were "only" breasts, but they were *my* breasts and to lose them would be to lose a part of myself.

The tenacious trio of fear, doubt, and worry were patiently waiting. Like vultures seeking that which is dead, they ruthlessly swept in when I allowed myself to wander from the sheltering wings of God's truths. I'm ashamed of how long I entertained them before I even recognized they were there. Previously won battles of the mind had taught me to act quickly, at the moment of recognition, and bring my thoughts under subjection. I had to actively choose to replace those thoughts with truths that I found in God's word.

Please don't misunderstand, this was not an overnight victory for me. I'm way too human for that. I shed many tears and sometimes felt as if the waves of despair would surely be my death. But as I continually submitted my thoughts to God and chose to meditate on the things instructed in His word I found that fear, doubt, and worry came less often and I recognized more quickly.

Treasure: Making choices based on Paul's checklist will help to guard your heart from the negative thoughts that Satan desires to use to overwhelm you. No matter how bleak your situation, choose which thoughts you will entertain based on Philippians 4:8. Using the criteria listed there to examine the music you hear, the books you read, the movies you watch, and the conversations in which you engage may not change your circumstance, but it will allow you to be victorious on the battle ground of your mind.

He made the laver of bronze and its base of bronze,
from the bronze mirrors of the serving women who
assembled at the door of the tabernacle of meeting.

Exodus 38:8

One month after the surgeon's knife removed the offending breast and its partner I started receiving radiation treatments - one treatment a day, five days a week for seven weeks. Although the radiation was no picnic, compared to what I had already endured it felt like being on vacation. Naps were a necessity and cold aloe vera gel was always on hand to help with the burn, but I was still able cook and clean. I could even drive myself to the hospital!

Follow up treatment (courtesy of the clinical trial) continued every three weeks for ten cycles. Thankfully this drug didn't wreak havoc on my body as some of the others had. Other than the inconvenience of tri-weekly hospital visits the journey's end was finally, blessedly realized. I continued to pray that I would miss none of the treasures that God had for me in that dark place named "cancer". So many of those precious gems were found right in the heart of darkness making me immediately aware of their truths, but I knew there would be more, carefully guarded by God and revealed in His perfect timing. Years later I'm still finding them.

One especially precious gem that I later discovered revealed to me the importance of allowing my image and identity to be rooted in Christ. Some truths can't be realized when you're too close to a situation. It's only after you've stepped away and your emotions have time to recuperate that you're able to clearly see what was there all along. This was one of those truths.

I'll have to take you all the way back to the

pre-cancer years to set the stage for the wonderful realization of this precious jewel. Before cancer, my life was completely wrapped up in my role as a wife and a mom. I understand that in certain circles of today's society that's frowned upon and some would probably feel that my life was lacking fulfillment. But I honestly loved being able to care for my family on a full time basis. Even in the mundane (How many times could one kid need a nose wiped in one day?), monotonous (We're having meatloaf *again*?), and maddening (How many times have I told you not to leave your shoes in the middle of the floor?) the ability to minister to my family brought me great joy. There were lots of snuggles with the little kids, late night talks with the older ones, homemade meals to ensure that my family was getting what they needed to be healthy. I really didn't mind getting up at 5:00 in the morning to make sure that Randy had a hot breakfast and a cup of coffee before he went to work.

Just as my actions exuded the fact that I was perfectly content with my profession, my outward image was that of femininity. I had thick, waist-length hair (not very stylish, but I loved it), curves (not necessarily in "all the right places", but curves nonetheless), nice fingernails, and long lashes that responded well to a nice coat of mascara.

Then came cancer and chemo and surgery and radiation. With no time to even process what was happening I was stripped of so many of the things that defined me as person. I was physically unable to prepare meals. The simple slip of a knife could quickly become a major issue because of bleeding issues and at times the nausea rendered me unable to even tolerate the smell of cooking food. I found myself unable to clean the house as side effects from the chemo made it impossible to properly grip a broom, mop, or vacuum cleaner. And always there was the incredible, overwhelming exhaustion. Just taking a load of clothes out of the washing machine would often necessitate a nap. Low white blood cell counts had my immune system so compromised that snuggling with runny-nosed little ones was a dangerous gamble. The older kids were cautious of robbing me of sleep with late night talks and their concern for causing me stress hindered them for sharing their heavy hearts. I was no longer able to fix Randy's breakfast or even wake up early enough to see him off to work. Intimate time was basically non-existent; I had so little left to give. My roles as nurturer, caregiver, homemaker and wife were horribly altered.

And let's not forget about my outward image. I was bald, my eyelashes were gone, my fingernails were rotted, my breasts removed and in their place nasty, ugly scars - forever reminders of a journey I did not choose for myself. "Feminine" was no longer an adjective I used to describe my appearance.

The attention demanded by the obvious effects of the uninvited disease was such that there was no time for analyzing or even recognizing anything that wasn't imperative for immediate survival. But sometimes in the quiet moments I would sense a just-under-the-surface disquiet that went beyond any words that I could form; an awareness that something deeper than the conspicuous was taking place. Looking back I realize that my soul was mourning the loss of my image. And months later I was still feeling the effects of that loss. Through prayer I felt the Holy Spirit speaking to me that, while there was nothing inherently wrong with the roles that I had filled or my pre-cancer appearance, those things should never have become my identity.

This treasure revealed to me that my identity is nothing outside of God. He is the only steadfast, never changing, always sure factor in our ever changing human lives. Every single situation we find ourselves in today has the potential to be drastically different tomorrow. Our jobs can be terminated, our spouse will one day pass away, our children will eventually leave home, and our health may falter. But a relationship with God, nurtured through reading His Word and prayer, will be the constant that can see us through any circumstance.

God showed me that it was no coincidence that Moses, according to His instructions, had the laver for His tabernacle constructed from the bronze mirrors (the reflection of an image) that belonged to the serving women. The laver was a place of cleansing, the place of preparation before entering the presence of God. It was symbolic of Jesus' cleansing blood. How amazing that thousands of years ago God chose to reveal in such a unique way that our image needs to be bathed in a relationship with Jesus Christ.

Treasure: When life's circumstances shift and our present roles change it's vital that who we are is rooted and grounded in Christ.

And God said to Moses, "I AM WHO I AM."
And He said, "Thus you shall say to the children of
Israel, 'I AM has sent me to you.'"

Exodus 3:14

Of all the journeys that have taken me into
dark places, the ones I've shared and the ones
whose details are still tucked away in a secret place
in my heart, I've found that every treasure I've
gleaned can be summed up in the words that God
spoke in Exodus 3:14. Whether the descent into
darkness was caused by unexpected tragedies or as
a direct result of my own sin and self-righteousness,
the truth of Exodus 3:14 stood as a steadfast

reminder of exactly who God is.

Even though I'd heard this passage preached more times than I could count and I'd read it on my own many times as well, I really didn't get it. The method that God chose to get Moses' attention or Moses' hesitation in accepting God's instruction was normally the topic of a pastor's message. On my own, I never really delved much deeper than the burning bush and the fact that it was having a holy conversation with Moses. The only thought that I had ever given to the words "I AM" was "Really?! Couldn't He be a bit more specific?"

God offered the words "I AM WHO I AM" in answer to a question being asked by Moses, a man who was simply minding his business and suddenly found himself being instructed (by a burning, non-consumed bush no less) to go to back to Egypt and lead the children of Israel out of slavery. Even though Moses had been away from Egypt for 40 years, he hadn't forgotten the stubbornness of the Israelites and I think he may have been a little nervous that they wouldn't follow him if he did decide to accept the quest. So he asks

God, "Who should I say sent me?" Now, this may seem like a silly question, but I can definitely relate. Just let one of my kids tell the other to go wash the dishes and I can promise you nobody's running to the kitchen, but if the instructions are given as "Mama said…" then some dishes are gonna be washed! Moses knew he better be going in with something more than just his own words.

God's reply to that most important of questions? "I AM WHO I AM… Thus you shall say to the children of Israel, 'I AM has sent me to you.'"

Those words seem so simplistic. But the very simplicity of those words begs us to grasp how all-encompassing they are. Sure, God could have thrown out a few of His titles; maybe, Jehovah Tsidkenu or Jehovah Jireh or Jehovah Shammah or any number of others, but instead He chose "I AM" because He is *everything* we need. Had He chosen to tell Moses exactly who He is Moses would still be recording the words centuries later. There is no limit to who our God is.

Treasure: HE IS enough. If you are afraid, HE IS Peace. If you are unemployed, HE IS Provision. Battling an addiction? HE IS Deliverance. Weary? HE IS Rest. Confused? HE IS Wisdom. I pray that you will take the time to search God's word and find that whatever you need, HE IS.

About the Author

Candy Reid, mom to 4 and wife to the love of her life, is a gifted encourager who seeks to seize every opportunity to inspire others in their walk with God.

A firm believer that the simple things in life are the most precious, Candy adores the sound of her children's laughter, coffee and conversation with a true-blue friend, and holding hands with her hubby on the backyard swing. And chocolate. Definitely chocolate.

You can contact her via email at: embracingthetrials@yahoo.com.

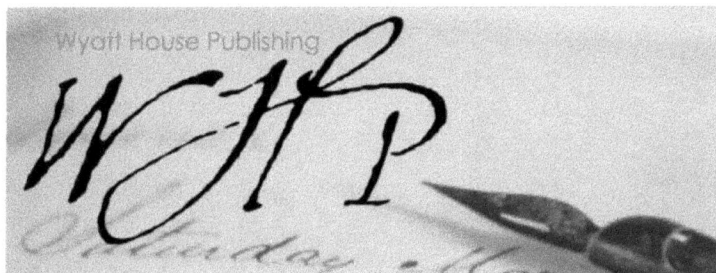

You have a story.
We want to publish it.

Everyone has as a story to tell. It might be about something you know how to do, or what has happened in your life, or it may be a thrilling, or romantic, or intriguing, or heartwarming, or suspenseful story, starring a cast of characters that have been swimming around in your imagination.

And at Wyatt House Publishing, we can get your story onto the pages of a book just like the one you are holding in your hand. With professional interior design and a custom, professionally designed cover built just for you from the start, you can finally see your dream of being an author become reality. Then, you will see your book listed with retailers all over the world as people are able to buy your book from wherever they are and have it delivered to their home or their e-reader.

So what are you waiting for? This is your time.

visit us at

www.wyattpublishing.com

for details on how to get started becoming a
published author right away.